Igor Stravinsky
Three Pieces
for Clarinet Solo

Revised Edition - 1993

This book © Copyright 1993 by Chester Music
ISBN 978-0-7119-2238-9
Order No.CH01551

Chester Music

Igor Stravinsky

3 PIECES FOR CLARINET SOLO

Igor Stravinsky wrote the *Three Pieces for Clarinet Solo* in Morges, 1918. The autograph title page gives: 'Musique pour Clarinette-solo et pour Werner Reinhart composée par Igor Strawinsky'.

The first edition was published by J. & W. Chester, Ltd. (London and Geneva), copyright 1920, plate number J.W.C.1151 (copy in the British Library). It gives the date of dedication as 1919. The first performance was given in Lausanne on 8th November 1919 by Edmond Allegra, who had played the important clarinet part in the first performance of *Histoire du Soldat* the previous year.

J.W.C.1151 contains numerous small additions when compared with the original manuscript: these include several of the dynamic markings, marks of articulation and breath marks. A number of such markings in the manuscript are not included in J.W.C.1151, or are contradicted.

No proofs or related correspondence from the composer appear to have survived. Thus we have to assume that J.W.C.1151 represents Stravinsky's final thoughts, particularly as he was apparently happy for the work to be reprinted unaltered for the rest of his life.

The edition was in fact printed nineteen times up to and including 1991, totalling nearly 30,000 copies. Remarkably, the only change in the musical text during these seventy years was the correction of the note values at III, bar 43, which was not done until the print of 1986.

This new edition (1993) is based on J.W.C.1151, with reference to the autograph. It aims to present a practical performance score, without excessive editorial presence: to have noted every minute difference between the two sources would have led to a very cluttered appearance. A few of the more interesting discrepancies have been recorded in footnotes.

J.W.C.1151 includes the following instruction:

Dans ces 3 pièces respecter toutes les respirations, les accents et le mouvement métronomique.

The breath marks, accents and metronome marks indicated in the 3 pieces should be strictly adhered to.

The breath marks are shown as commas: it is not clear whether these should or should not interfere with the rhythmic pulse. The editor prefers the latter, i.e. if there is no rest shown, the breath should be taken out of the previous note.

Nicholas Hare
St. Albans 1993

THREE PIECES

for Clarinet Solo

IGOR STRAVINSKY (1882-1971)

Edited by Nicholas Hare

Molto tranquillo ♩=52 I

sempre *p*

poco più mosso

lunga

poco più *f*

* Sur la clarinette Boehm prendre ce fa♯ avec l'auriculaire de la main gauche.
On the Boehm clarinet play this F♯ with the little finger of the left hand.

Clarinette en la de préférence
Preferably Clarinet in A

ritardando (poco)

sombrer le son
subito meno f

1. MS has *mp*

5. MS has 8/16 [notation] with time signature altered to 4/16 ;

JWC 1151 has the ambiguous 4/16 [notation] , altered to 4/16 [notation] in the 1986 reprint.

6. MS has [notation]

7. MS has [notation] *sf*

7